EASY GUITAR

Harvest Neil Young

CONTENTS

ISBN: 978-1-4803-4158-6

HAL•LEONARD®
CORPORATION
7777 W. BLUEMOUND RD. P.O. BOX 13819 MILWAUKEE, WI 53213

Out on the Weekend

Think I'll pack it in and buy a pick-up
Take it down to LA
Find a place to call my own and try to fix up.
Start a brand new day. ___

The woman I'm thinkin of — she loved me all up
But I'm so down today
She's so fine she's in my mind. I hear her callin. ___

See the lonely boy, out on the week-end
Trying to make it pay.
Can't relate to joy, He tries to speak and
Can't begin to say. ___

She got pictures on the wall - They make me look up
From her big brass bed.
Now I'm running down the road trying to stay up
somewhere in her head. ___

Out on the Weekend

Words and Music by Neil Young

Strum Pattern: 1
Pick Pattern: 5

but I'm so down___ to - day.

She's so fine, she's in my mind,

I hear her call - in':

Chorus

See the lone - ly boy___

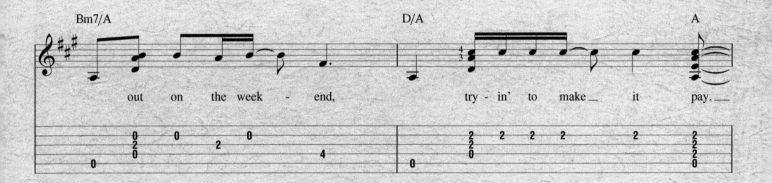

out on the week - end,

try - in' to make___ it pay.___

Can't re - late___ to joy,___

he tries to speak and

2nd time, D.S. and fade

can't be - gin to say.___

Harvest

Did I see you down in a young girls town
With your mother in so much pain?
I was almost there at the top of the stairs
With her screamin' in the rain.
Did she wake you up to tell you that
It was only a change of plan?
Dream up, Dream up, Let me fill your cup
With the promise of a man.

Did I see you walking with the boys
Though it was not hand in hand?
And was some black face in a lonely place
When you could understand?
Did she wake you up to tell you that
It was only a change of plan?
Dream up, Dream up, Let me fill your cup
With the promise of a man.
—

Will I see you give more than I can take?
Will I only harvest some?
As the days fly past will we lose our grasp
Or fuse it in the sun?
Did she wake you up to tell you that
It was only a change of plan?
Dream up, Dream up, Let me fill your cup
With the promise of a man.
—

Harvest

Words and Music by Neil Young

A Man Needs a Maid

I was thinking that maybe I'd get a maid
Find a place nearby for her to stay.
Just someone to keep my house clean —
Fix my meals and go away.
A maid — A man needs a maid.

To give a love, you gotta live a love.
To live a love, you gotta be part of.
When will I see you again?

A while ago somewhere I don't know when
I was watching a movie with a friend.
I fell in love with the actress.
She was playing a part that I could understand —
A maid. A man needs a maid.

When will I see you again?

A Man Needs a Maid

Words and Music by Neil Young

Interlude

*Orchestra arr. for gtr., next 8 meas.

It's

Bridge

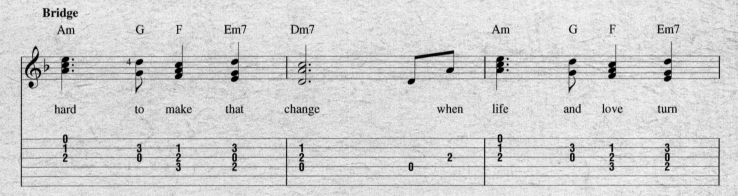

hard to make that change when life and love turn

strange and old.   To

give a love,   you got - ta live a love.

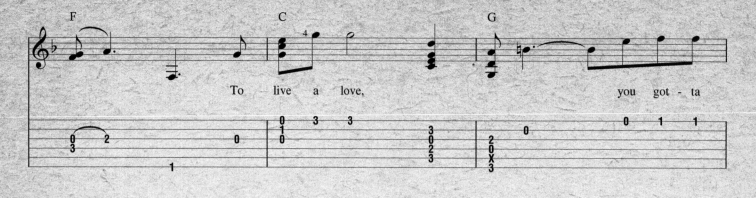

To live a love, you got-ta

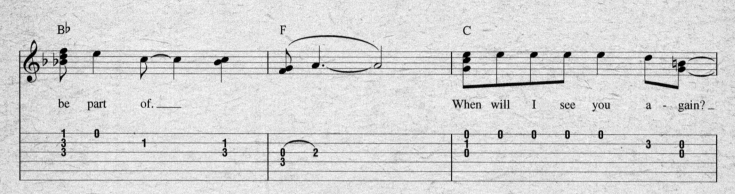

be part of.____ When will I see you a - gain?__

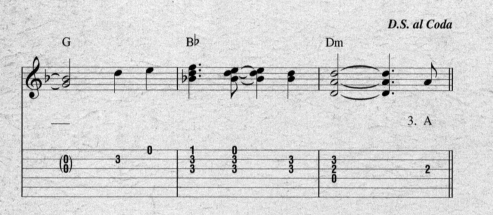

D.S. al Coda

3. A

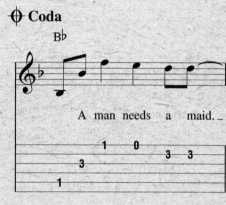

Coda

A man needs a maid.__

Outro

*Orchestra arr. for gtr., next 6 meas.

When will I see you a - gain?___

Heart of Gold

I want to live
I want to give
I've been a miner for a heart of gold
Its these expressions I never give
That keep me searching for a heart of gold
And I'm getting old.
—

I've been to Hollywood
I've been to Redwood
I crossed the ocean for a heart of gold
I've been in my mind, Its such a fine line
That keeps me searching for a Heart of Gold
And I'm getting old. —

Heart of Gold

Words and Music by Neil Young

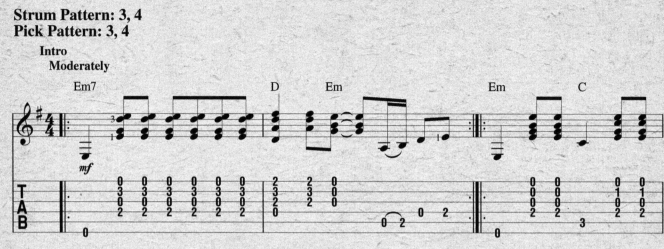

Strum Pattern: 3, 4
Pick Pattern: 3, 4

Intro
Moderately

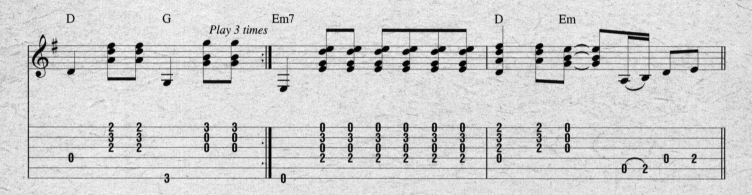

Play 3 times

Verse

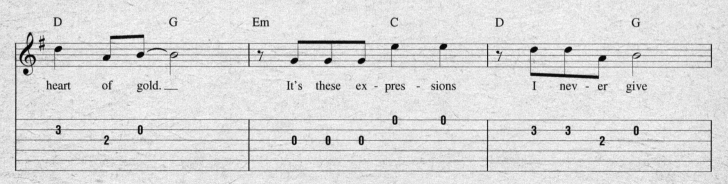

1. I wan-na live, I wan-na give, I've been a min-er for a
2. *See additional lyrics*

heart of gold. ___ It's these ex-pres - sions I nev-er give

that keep me search-in' for a heart of gold,_____ and I'm get-tin' old.___

Keep me search-in' for a heart of gold,_____

and I'm get-tin' old._____

Interlude

Additional Lyrics

2. I've been to Hollywood, I've been to Redwood.
   I'd cross the ocean for a heart of gold.
   I've been in my mind. It's such a fine line
   That keeps me searchin' for a heart of gold,
   And I'm gettin' old.
   Keeps me searchin' for a heart of gold,
   And I'm gettin' old.

Are you ready for the Country?

Slipping and sliding and playing domino
Lefting and then Righting, it's not a crime you know.
You gotta tell your story boy, Before its time to go.
Are you ready for the country because its time to go?

—

I was talkin to the preacher — said god was on my side.
Then I ran into the hangman — he said "its time to die"
You gotta tell your story boy. You know the reason why.

Are you ready for the Country — Because its time to go.

Are You Ready for the Country?

Words and Music by Neil Young

Old Man

Old man look at my life. I'm a lot like you were.
Old man look at my life - twenty four and there's so much more
Live alone in a paradise that makes me think of two.
Love lost, such a cost, Give me things that don't get lost.
Like a coin that won't get tossed
Rolling Home to you.

Old man take a look at my life
I'm a lot like you.
I need someone to love me the whole day through
Ah, one look in my eyes and you can tell that's true.

Lullabys, look in your eyes, run around the same old town.
Doesn't mean that much to me to mean that much to you.
I've been first and last, look at how the time goes past.
But I'm all alone at last.
Rolling home to you.

Old Man

Words and Music by Neil Young

Strum Pattern: 3, 4
Pick Pattern: 3, 4

Intro
Moderately, in 2

let ring throughout

*2nd time, bass plays F.

Pre-Verse

Old man, look at my life,

I'm a lot like you were. _____ Old man, look at my life,

I'm a lot like you were. _____

Verse

1. Old man, look at my life, twen-ty-four and there's so much more.
2. *See additional lyrics*

Live a-lone in a par-a-dise that makes me think of two.

Love lost, such a cost, give me things that don't get lost,

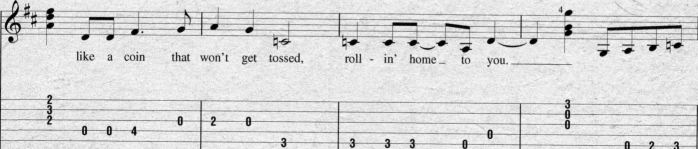

like a coin that won't get tossed, roll-in' home to you.

* Roll 3rd finger.

Chorus

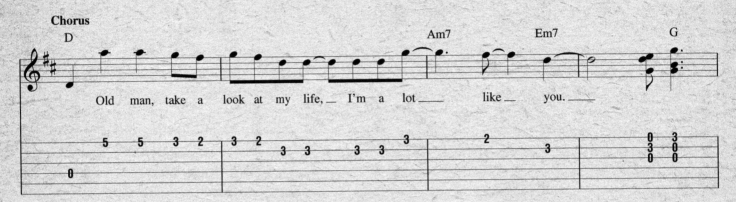

Old man, take a look at my life, __ I'm a lot __ like __ you. __

I need some-one to love __ me the whole __ day __ through. __

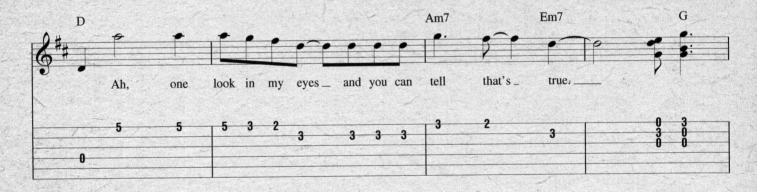

Ah, one look in my eyes __ and you can tell that's __ true. __

1.

Additional Lyrics

2. Lullabys look in your eyes, run around the same old town,
Doesn't mean that much to me to mean that much to you.
I've been first and last, look at how the time goes past,
But I'm all alone at last, rollin' home to you.

There's a World

There's a world you're living in
No one else has your part
All god's children in the wind
Take it in and blow hard

Look around you — Has it found you walking down the avenue?
See what it brings — Could be good things in the air for you.

We are leaving. We are gone.
Come with us to all alone.
Never worry. Never moan.
We will leave you all alone.

In the mountains, in the cities, You can see the dream.
Look around you. Has it found you? Is it what it seems?

There's a world you're living in
No one else has your part.
All god's children in the wind
Take it in and blow hard.

There's a World

Words and Music by Neil Young

Strum Pattern: 3
Pick Pattern: 3

Look a - round it.
In the moun - tains

Have you found it
in the cit - ies,

walk - in' down the av -
you can see the dream.

- e - nue?

See what it brings,
Look a - round you.

could be good things
Has it found you?

in the air for you.
Is it what for it seems?

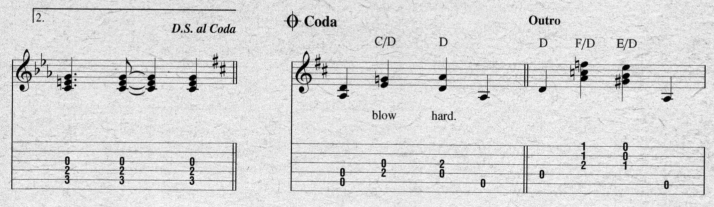

D.S. al Coda

Coda

C/D   D   D   F/D   E/D

blow   hard.

Outro

C/D   D   F/D   E/D   C/D   D

rit.

Alabama

Oh Alabama, the devil fools with the best laid plan.
Swing low Alabama.
You got the spare change – you got to feel strange
And now the moment is all that it meant.
Alabama – you got the weight on your shoulders
Thats breaking your back.
Your cadillac has got a wheel in the ditch
And a wheel on the track

Oh Alabama, Banjos playing thru the broken glass
Windows down in Alabama
See the old folks tied in white ropes
Hear the banjo. Don't it take you down home?

Oh Alabama, Can I see you and shake your hand
Make friends down in Alabama.
I'm from a new land
I come to you and see all this ruin
What are you doing Alabama?
You got the rest of the union to help you along
Whats going wrong?

Alabama

Words and Music by Neil Young

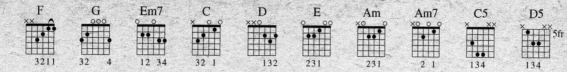

Strum Pattern: 1
Pick Pattern: 5

Intro
Slow

Verse

1. Oh, _____ Al - a - bam - a,
3. *Instrumental*

the dev - il fools with the best laid plan. Swing low, _____ Al - a - bam-

Pre-Chorus

You got the spare change, you got to feel strange,

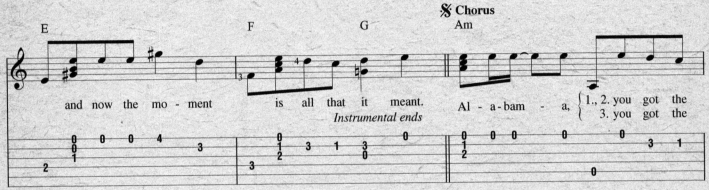

and now the mo - ment is all that it meant. Al - a - bam - a,

Instrumental ends

1., 2. you got the
3. you got the

To Coda

weight on your shoul - ders that's break - in' your back.
rest of the Un - ion to help you a - long.

Your
What's

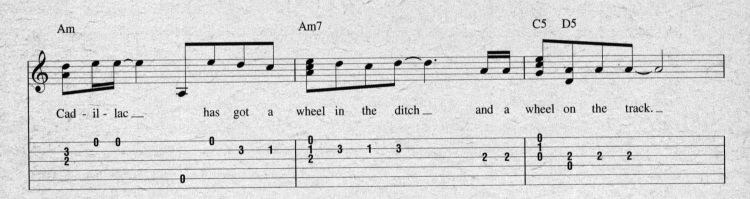

Cad - il - lac has got a wheel in the ditch and a wheel on the track.

Verse

2. Oh, Al - a - bam - a,
4. Oh, Al - a - bam - a,

The Needle and the Damage Done

I caught you knocking at my cellar door.
I love you baby "Can I have some more"
Oh the damage done.
I hit the city and I lost my band.
I watched the needle take another man
Gone. The damage done

I sing the song because I love the man
I know that some of you don't understand
Milk-blood to keep from running out

I've seen the needle and the damage done
A little part of it in everyone.
But every junkies like a setting sun

The Needle and the Damage Done

Words and Music by Neil Young

Additional Lyrics

2. I hit the city and I lost my band.
   I watched the needle take another man.
   Gone, gone, the damage done.

4. I've seen the needle and the damage done.
   A little part of it in ev'ry one.
   But ev'ry junkie's like a setting sun.

Words

Someone and someone were down by the pond
Looking for something to plant in the lawn.
Out in the fields they were turning the soil
I'm sitting here hoping this water will boil
When I look thru the window and out on the road
They're bringing me presents and saying hello.
Singing Words — Words between the lines of age

If I was a junkman selling you cars,
Washing your windows and shining your stars,
Thinking your mind was my own in a dream
What would you wonder and how would it seem?
Living in castles a bit at a time
The King started laughing and talking in rhyme.
Singing Words — Words between the lines of age.

Words (Between the Lines of Age)

Words and Music by Neil Young

*Strum Pattern: 7
*Pick Pattern: 7

Intro
Moderately

*Combine Patterns 7 & 10 for   meas.

Verse

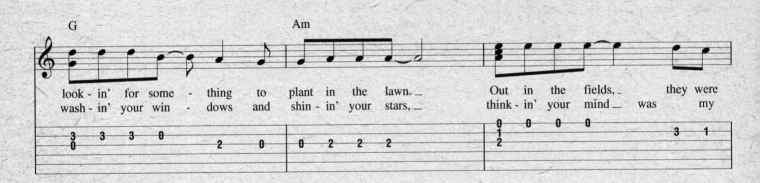

1. Some - one and some - one were down by the pond ___
2. If I was a junk ___ man sell - in' you cars, ___

**Use Pattern 6.

look - in' for some - thing to plant in the lawn. ___ Out in the fields, ___ they were
wash - in' your win - dows and shin - in' your stars, ___ think - in' your mind ___ was my

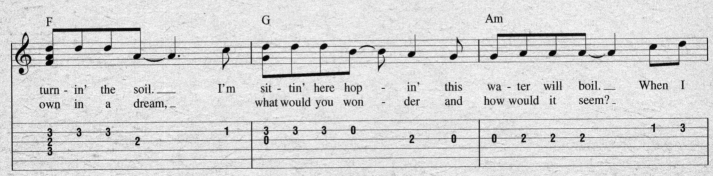

turn - in' the soil. ___ I'm sit - tin' here hop - in' this wa - ter will boil. ___ When I
own in a dream, ___ what would you won - der and how would it seem? ___

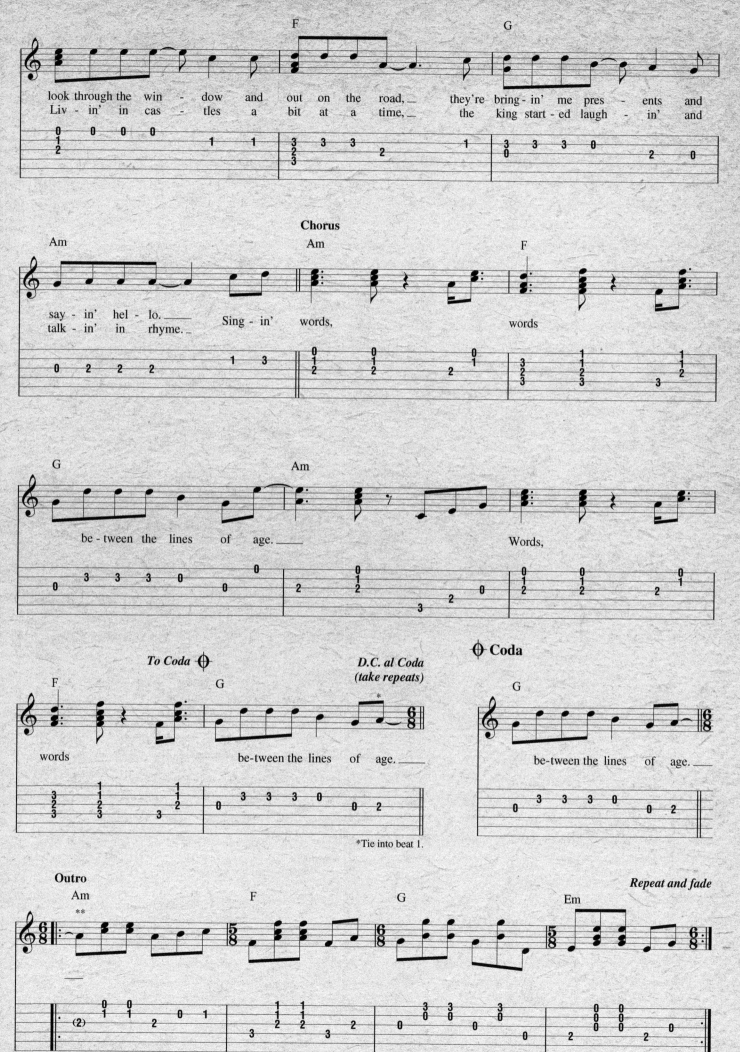

STRUM AND PICK PATTERNS

This chart contains the suggested strum and pick patterns that are referred to by number at the beginning of each song in this book. The symbols ⊓ and ∨ in the strum patterns refer to down and up strokes, respectively. The letters in the pick patterns indicate which right-hand fingers play which strings.

p = thumb
i = index finger
m = middle finger
a = ring finger

For example; Pick Pattern 2
is played: thumb - index - middle - ring

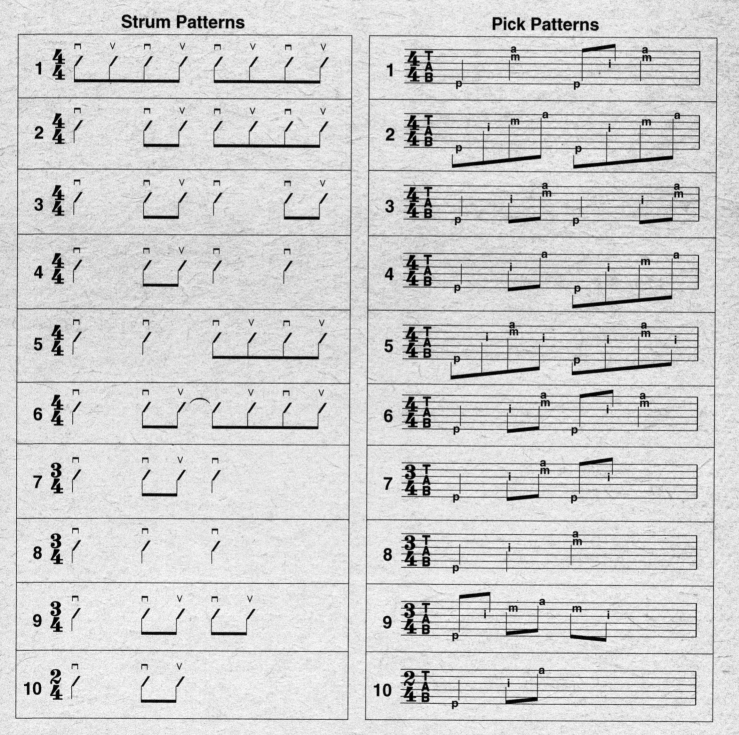

You can use the 3/4 Strum and Pick Patterns in songs written in compound meter (6/8, 9/8, 12/8, etc.).
For example, you can accompany a song in 6/8 by playing the 3/4 pattern twice in each measure.
The 4/4 Strum and Pick Patterns can be used for songs written in cut time (¢) by doubling the note time values in the patterns. Each pattern would therefore last two measures in cut time.

1. **Out On The Weekend†**
(with the Stray Gators)

2. **Harvest†**
(with the Stray Gators)

3. **A Man Needs A Maid°**
(with the London Symphony Orchestra
Conducted by David Meecham
Arranged by Jack Nitzsche)

4. **Heart Of Gold†**
(with the Stray Gators/additional
vocals by James Taylor & Linda Rondstadt)

5. **Are You Ready For The Country?†**
(with the Stray Gators/additional
vocals by David Crosby & Graham Nash)

6. **Old Man†**
(with the Stray Gators/additional
vocals by James Taylor & Linda Rondstadt)

7. **There's A World°**
(with the London Symphony Orchestra
Conducted by David Meecham
Arranged by Jack Nitzsche)

8. **Alabama†**
(with the Stray Gators/additional
vocals by David Crosby & Graham Nash)

9. **The Needle And The Damage Done§**
(live at Royce Hall – UCLA)

10. **Words (Between The Lines Of Age)†**
(with the Stray Gators/additional
vocals by Stephen Stills & Graham Nash)

† Produced by Elliot Mazer & Neil Young
° Produced by Jack Nitzsche
§ Produced by Neil Young & Henry Lewy

Stray Gators:
Ben Keith – Pedal Steel Guitar & Dobro
Kenny Buttrey – Drums
Tim Drummond – Bass
Jack Nitzsche – Piano & Lap Slide Guitar
John Harris –(Piano on Harvest)
Teddy Irwin – (Guitar on Heart of Gold)
James McMahon – (Piano on Old Man)
James Taylor – (Banjo Guitar on Old Man)

Recorded at:
Quadrafonic Sound Studios – Nashville, Tenn.
Broken Arrow Studio #2 – California
Barking Town Hall – London, England
Royce Hall-UCLA – California
Mastered by Chris Bellman at Bernie Grundman Mastering

All songs written by Neil Young
Design by Tom Wilkes for Camouflage Productions
Photography by Joel Bernstein
Special thanks to David & Elliot

Inspired by the original songbook.
Songbook Art Direction & Design: Gary Burden and Jenice Heo for R Twerk & Co
Songbook Production Design: Jesse Burden